Illustrations copyright © 2020 by James Christopher Carroll

Edited by Amy Novesky and Kate Riggs \ Designed by Rita Marshall

Published in 2020 by Creative Editions   P. O. Box 227, Mankato, MN 56002 USA

Creative Editions is an imprint of The Creative Company www.thecreativecompany.us

Library of Congress Cataloging-in-Publication Data

Names: Whitman, Walt, author. / Carroll, James Christopher, illustrator.

Title: The world below the brine / by Walt Whitman; illustrated by James Christopher Carroll.

Summary: Nineteenth-century poet Walt Whitman employs the language of his day

to express a wonder about the world below the sea that is timeless.

Identifiers: LCCN 2019056646 / ISBN 978-1-56846-361-2

Subjects: LCSH: Marine biology—Juvenile poetry. / Children's poetry, American.

Classification: LCC PS3222.W6 2020   DDC 811/.3—dc23

First edition 9 8 7 6 5 4 3 2 1

Walt Whitman illustrated by James Christopher Carroll

THE WORLD
BELOW THE BRINE

Creative Editions

The world below the brine,

Forests at the bottom of the sea, the branches and leaves,

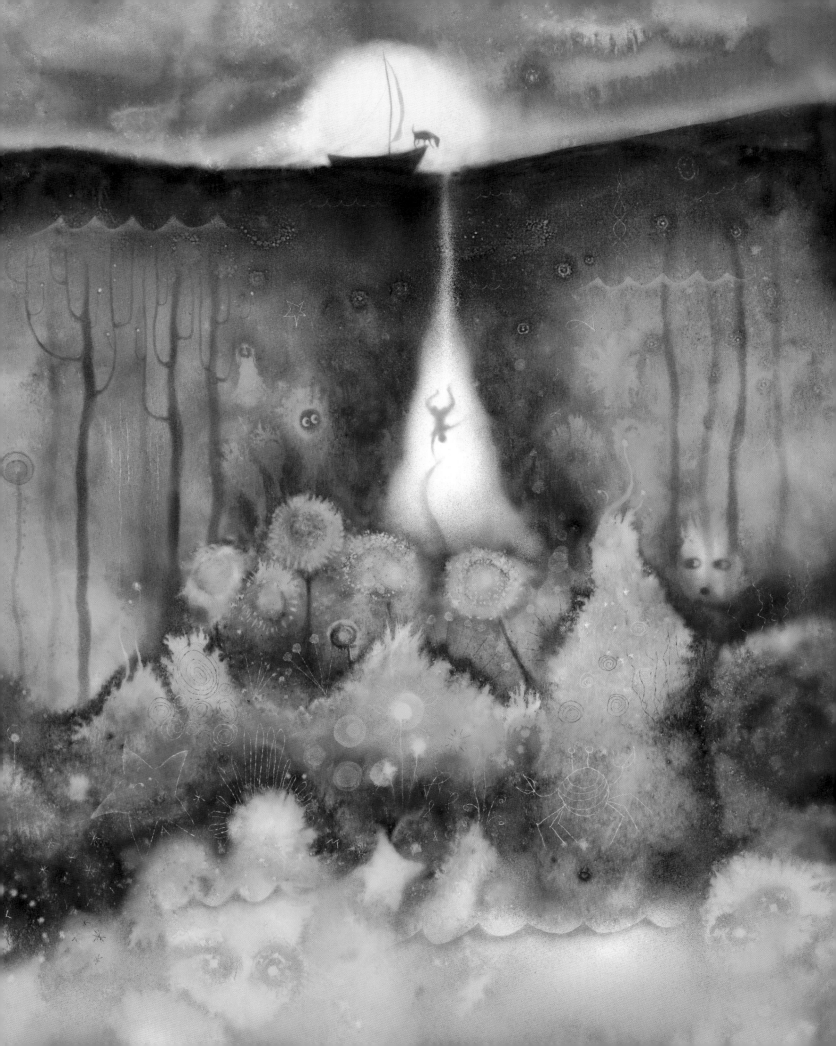

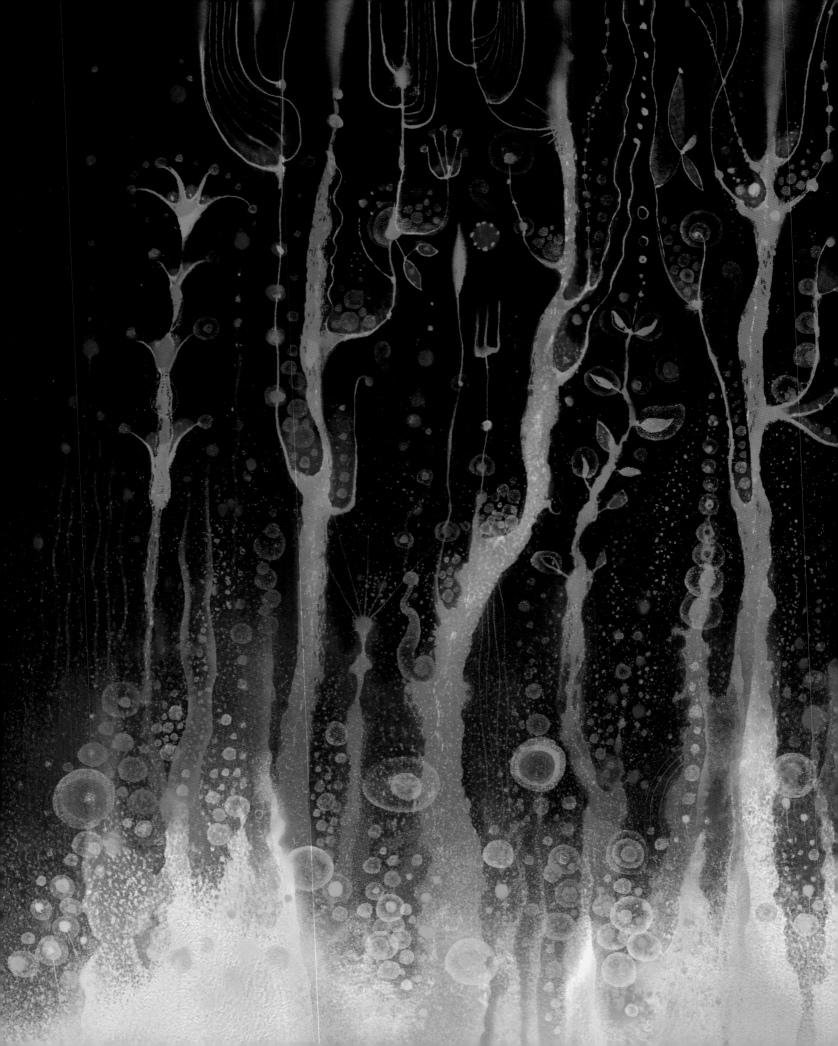

Sea-lettuce, vast lichens, strange flowers
and seeds, the thick tangle, openings,
and pink turf,

Different colors, pale gray and green, purple, white, and gold, the play of light through the water,

Dumb swimmers there among the rocks, coral, gluten, grass, rushes, and the aliment of the swimmers,

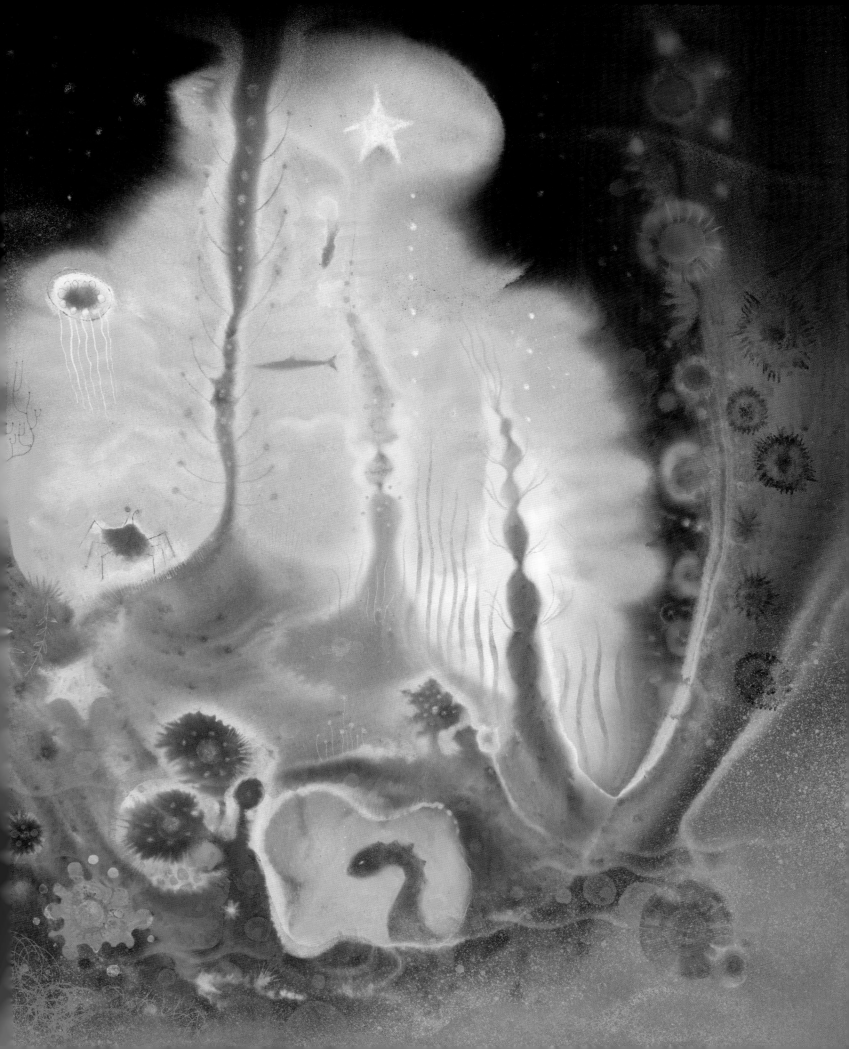

Sluggish existences grazing there
suspended, or slowly crawling
close to the bottom,

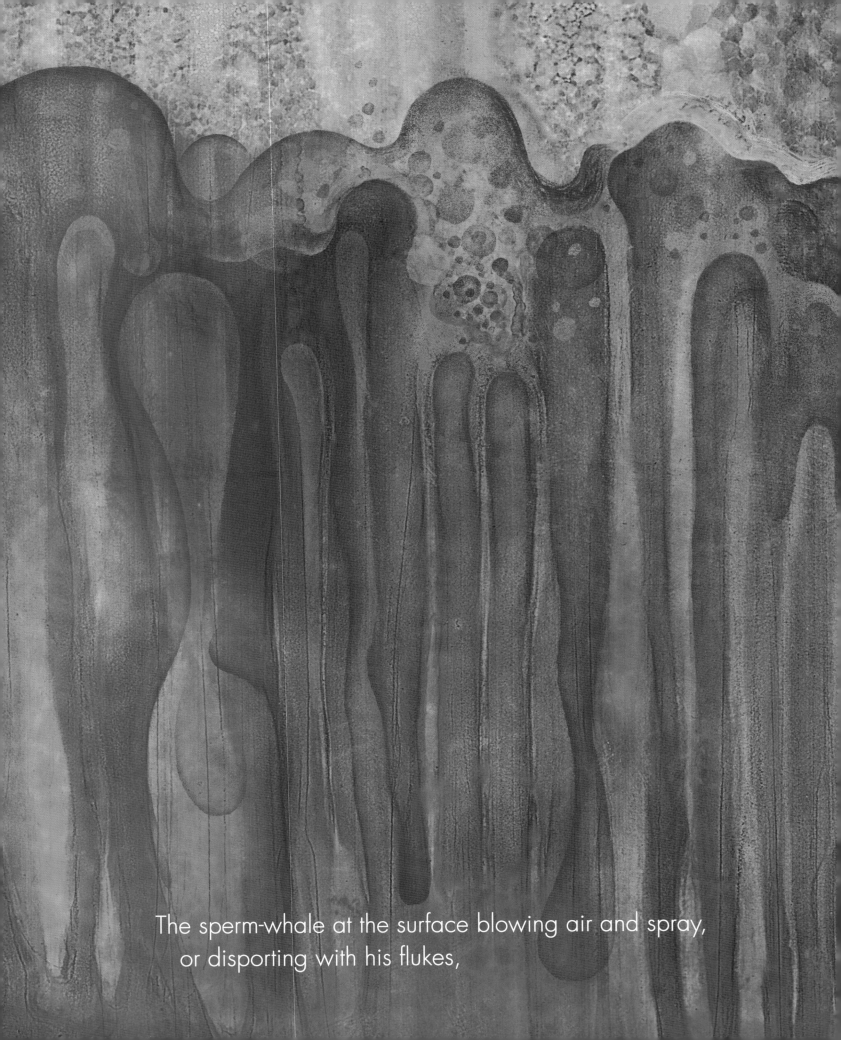

The sperm-whale at the surface blowing air and spray,
or disporting with his flukes,

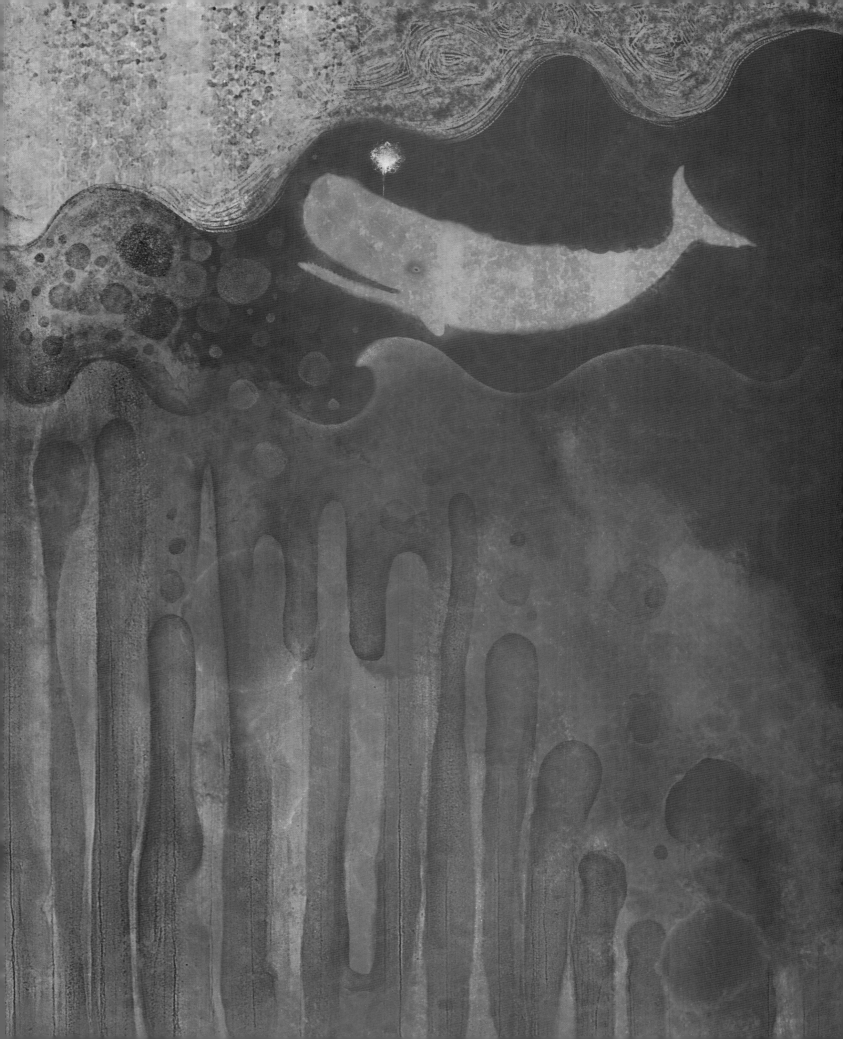

The leaden-eyed shark, the walrus, the turtle,
the hairy sea-leopard, and the sting-ray,

Passions there, wars, pursuits, tribes, sight in those ocean-depths,
breathing that thick-breathing air, as so many do,

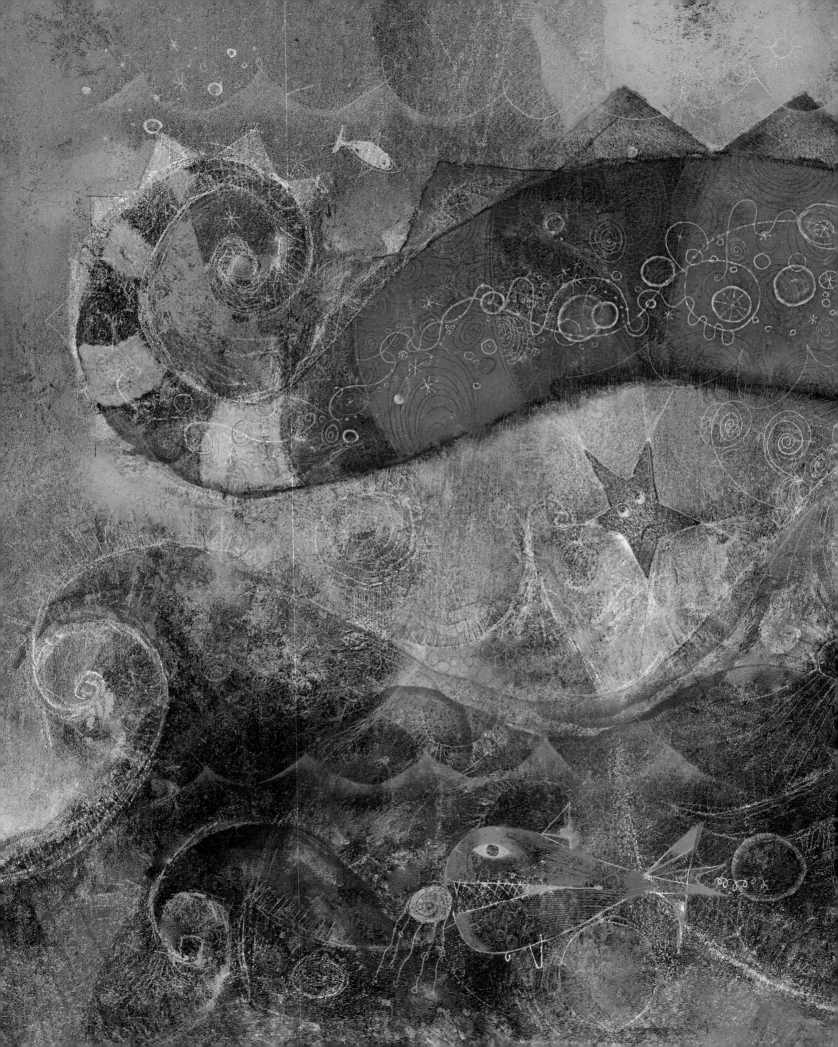

The change thence to the sight here,

and to the subtle air breathed by beings
like us who walk this sphere,

The change onward
from ours to that of beings
who walk other
spheres.